POPULAR TALES

Coloring Book

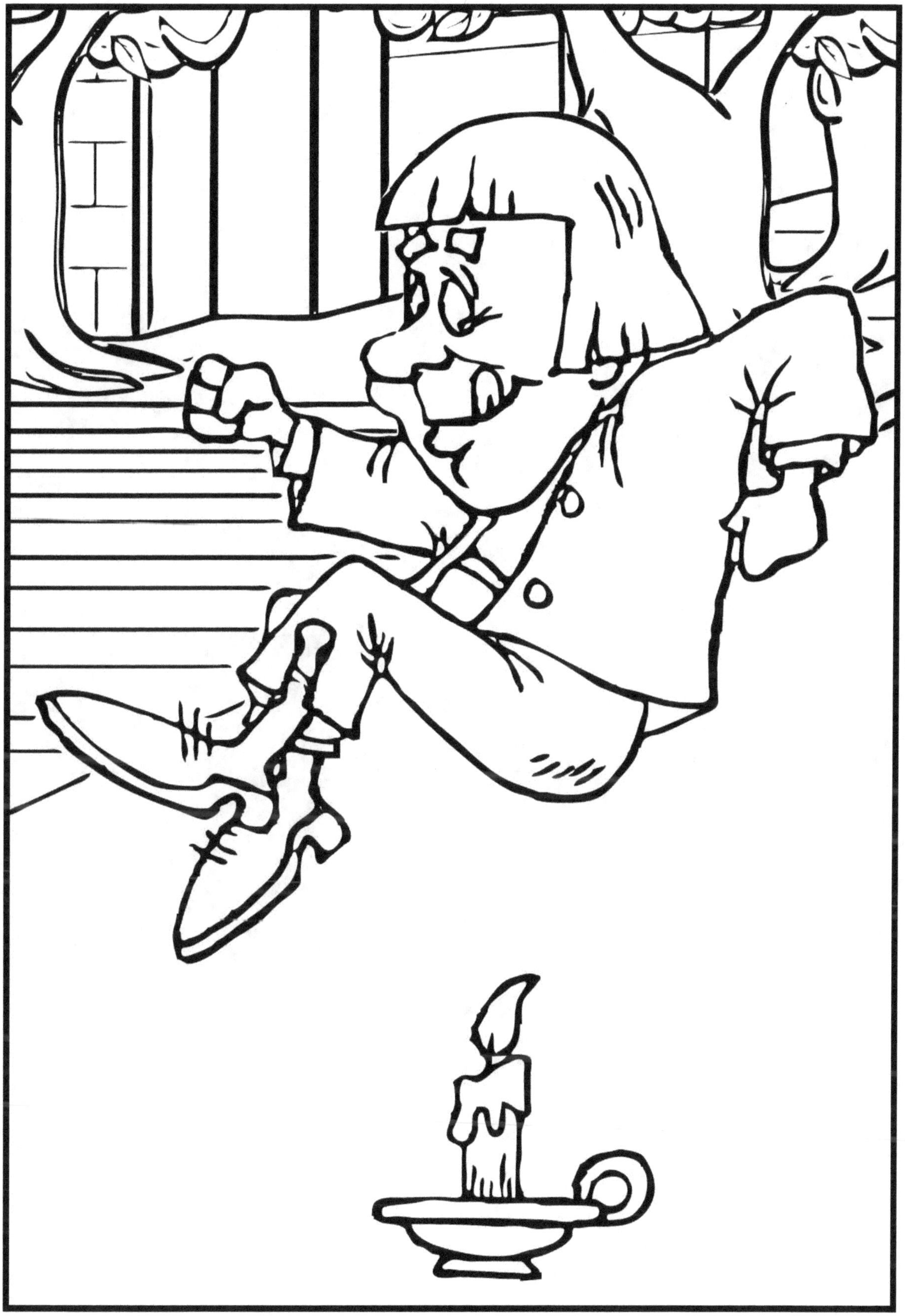

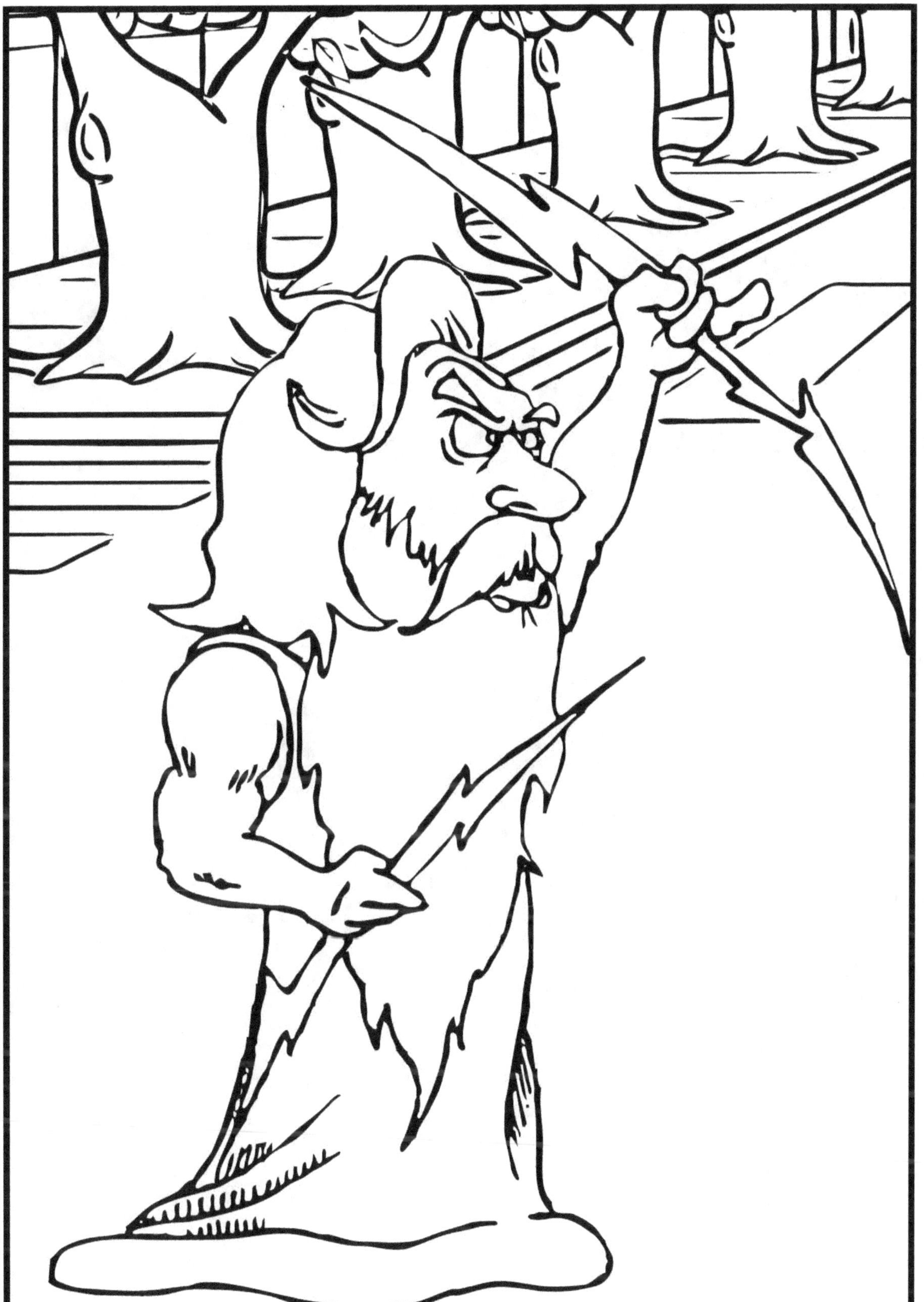

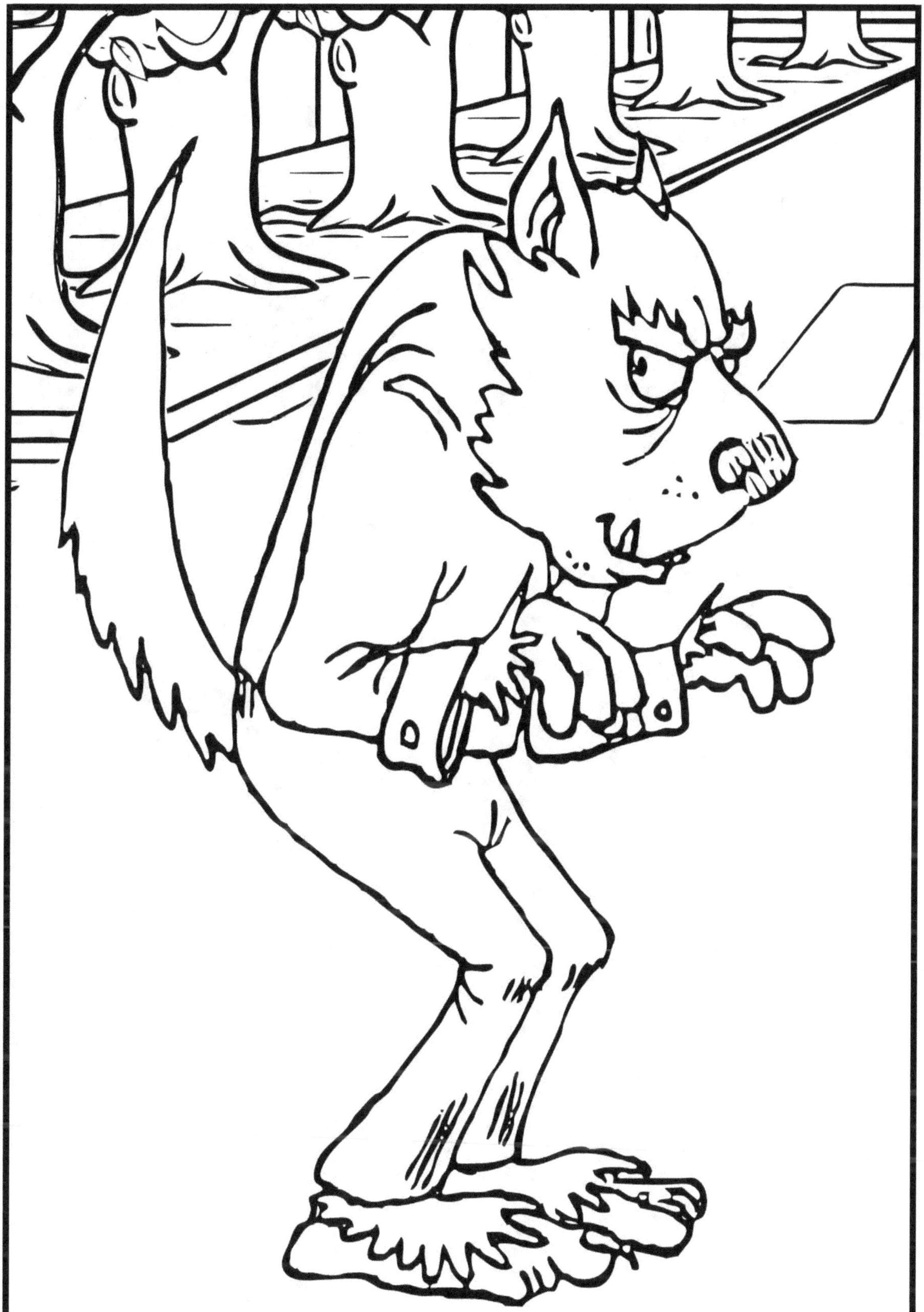

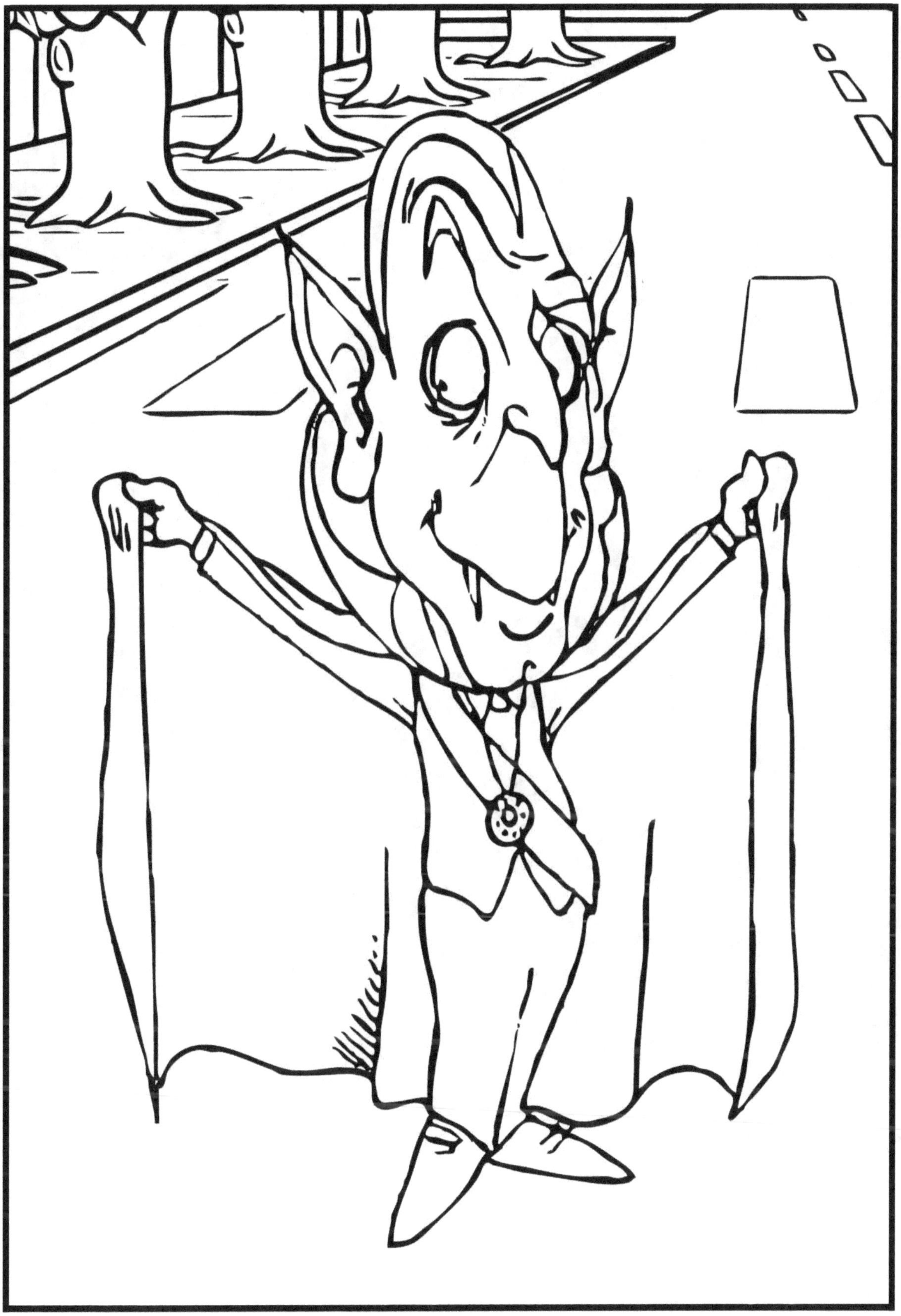

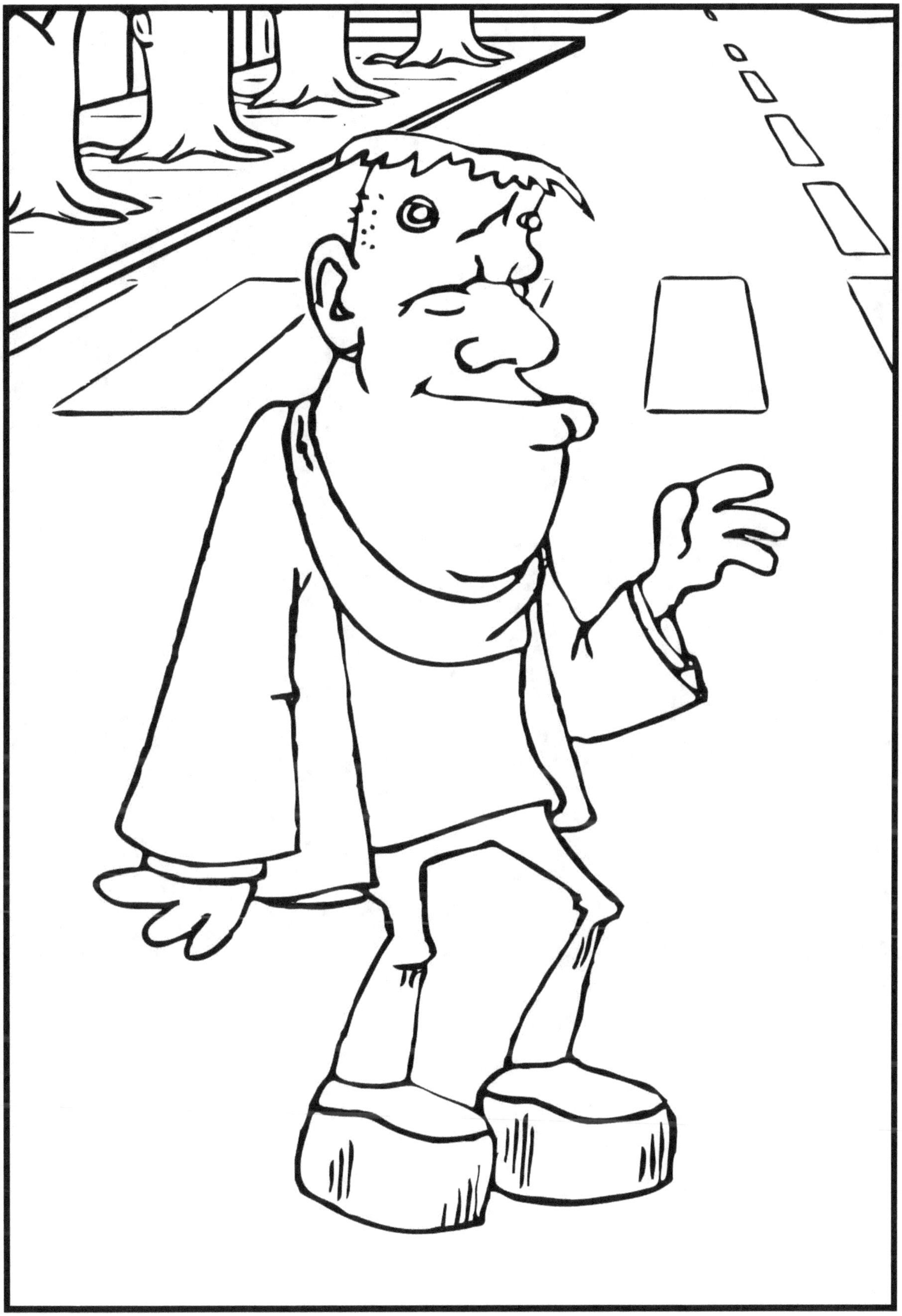

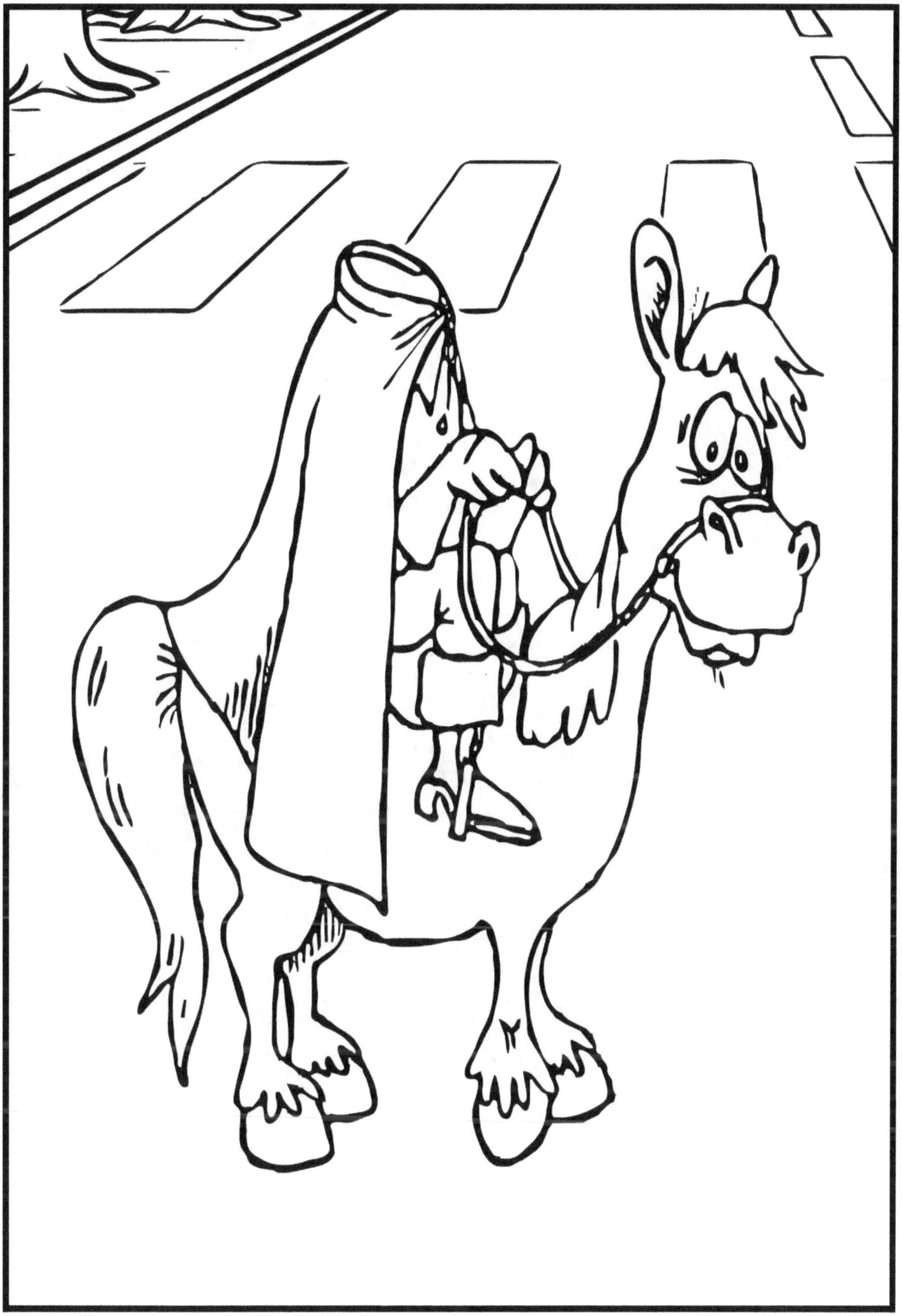

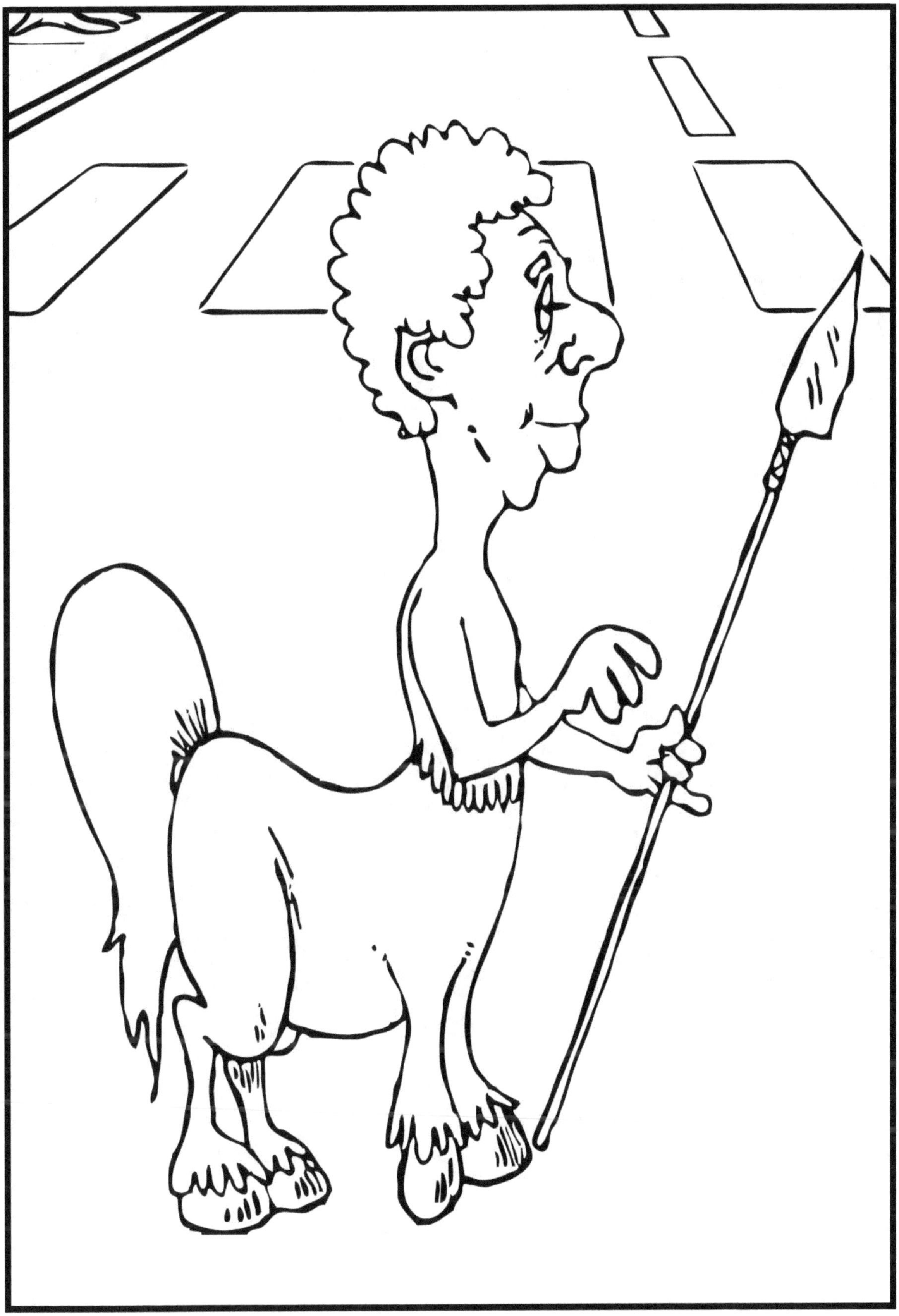

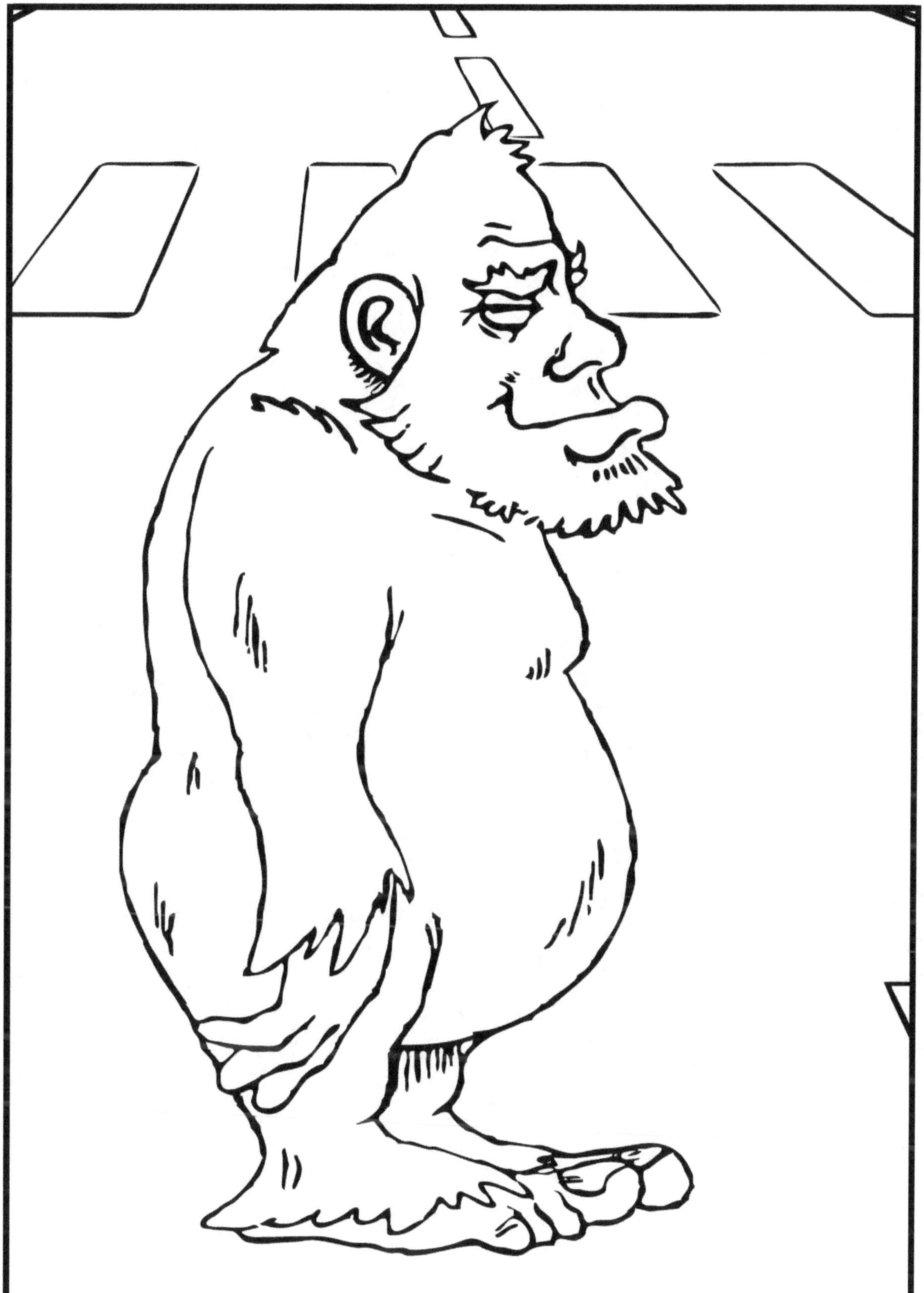

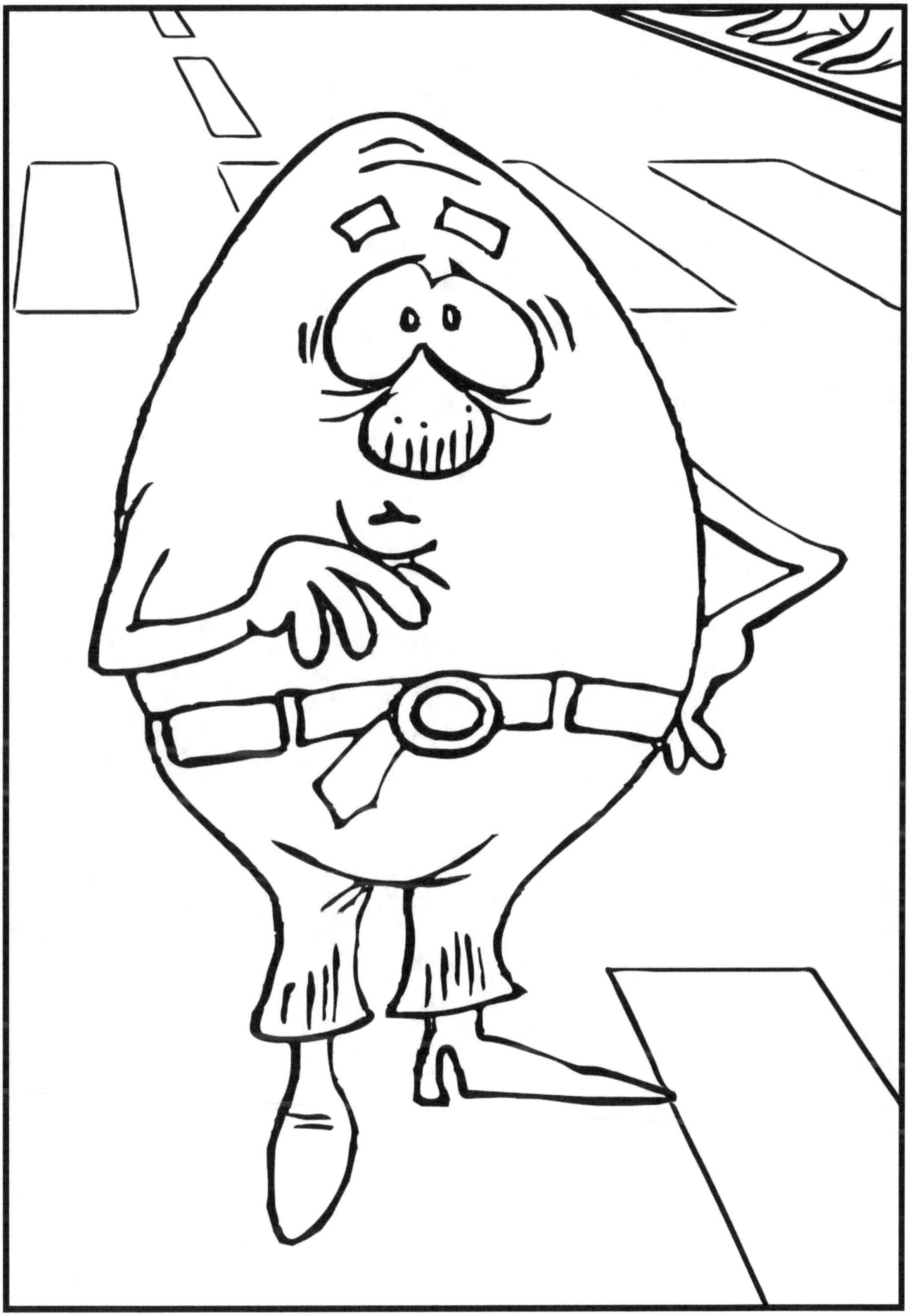

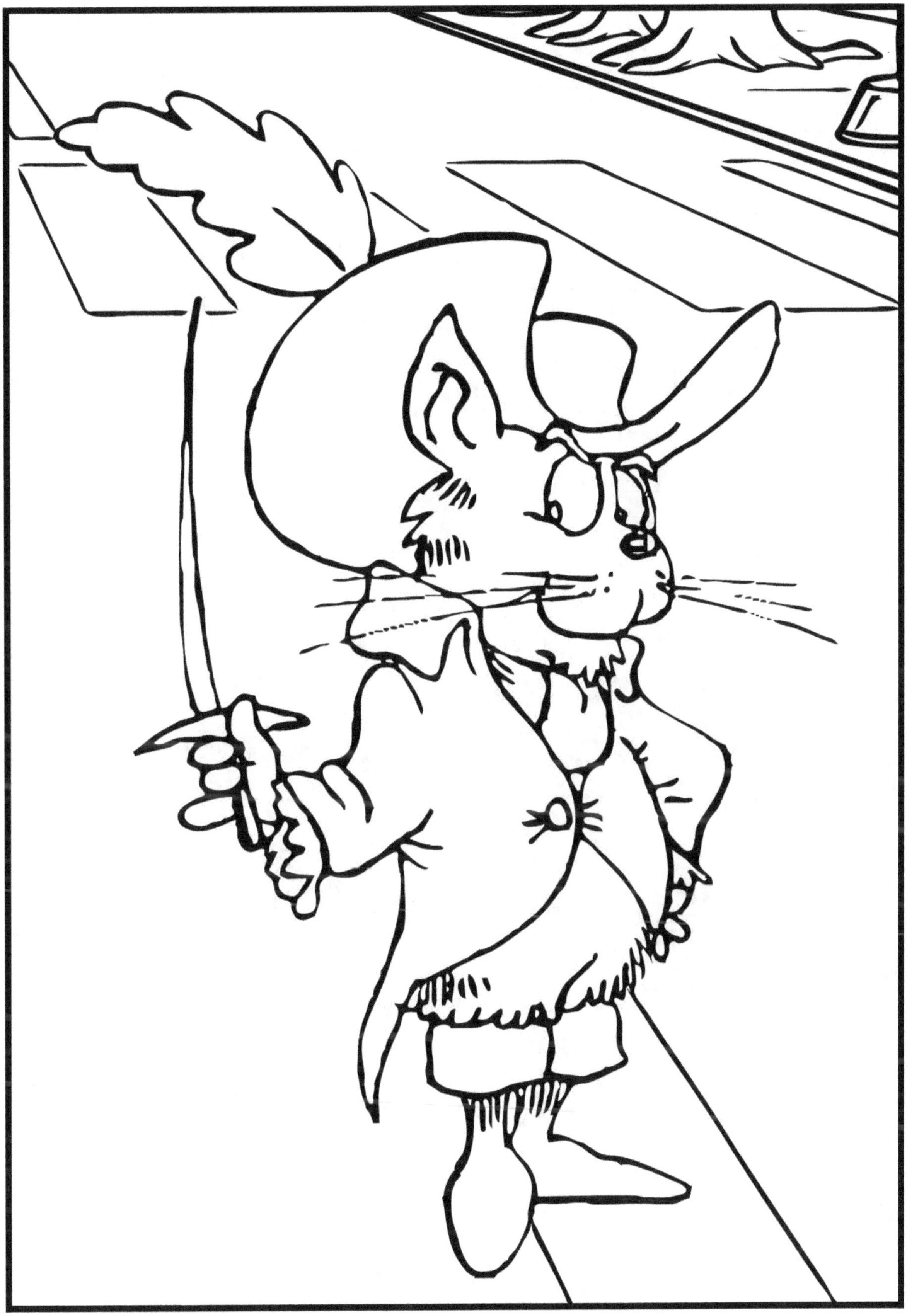

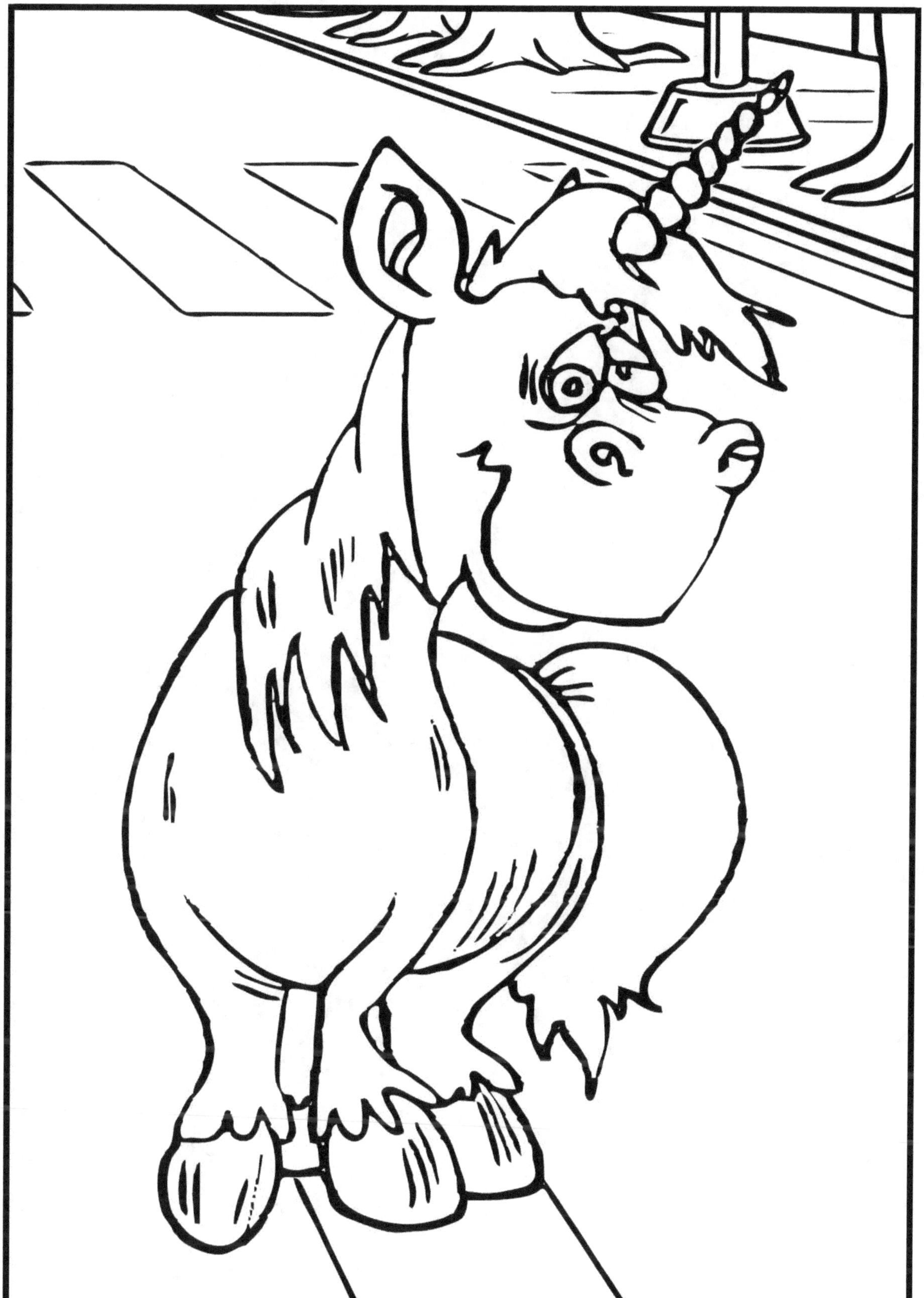

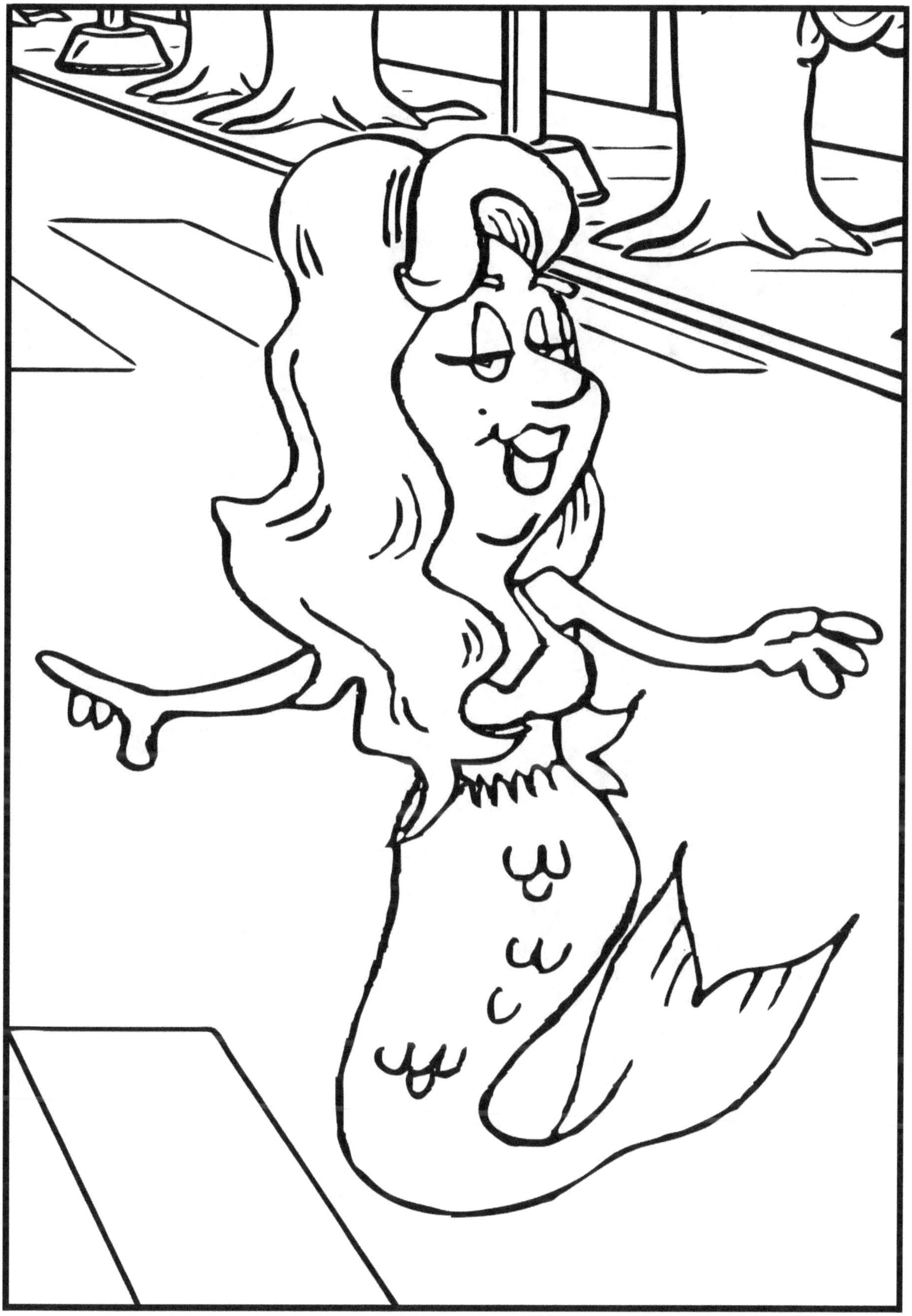

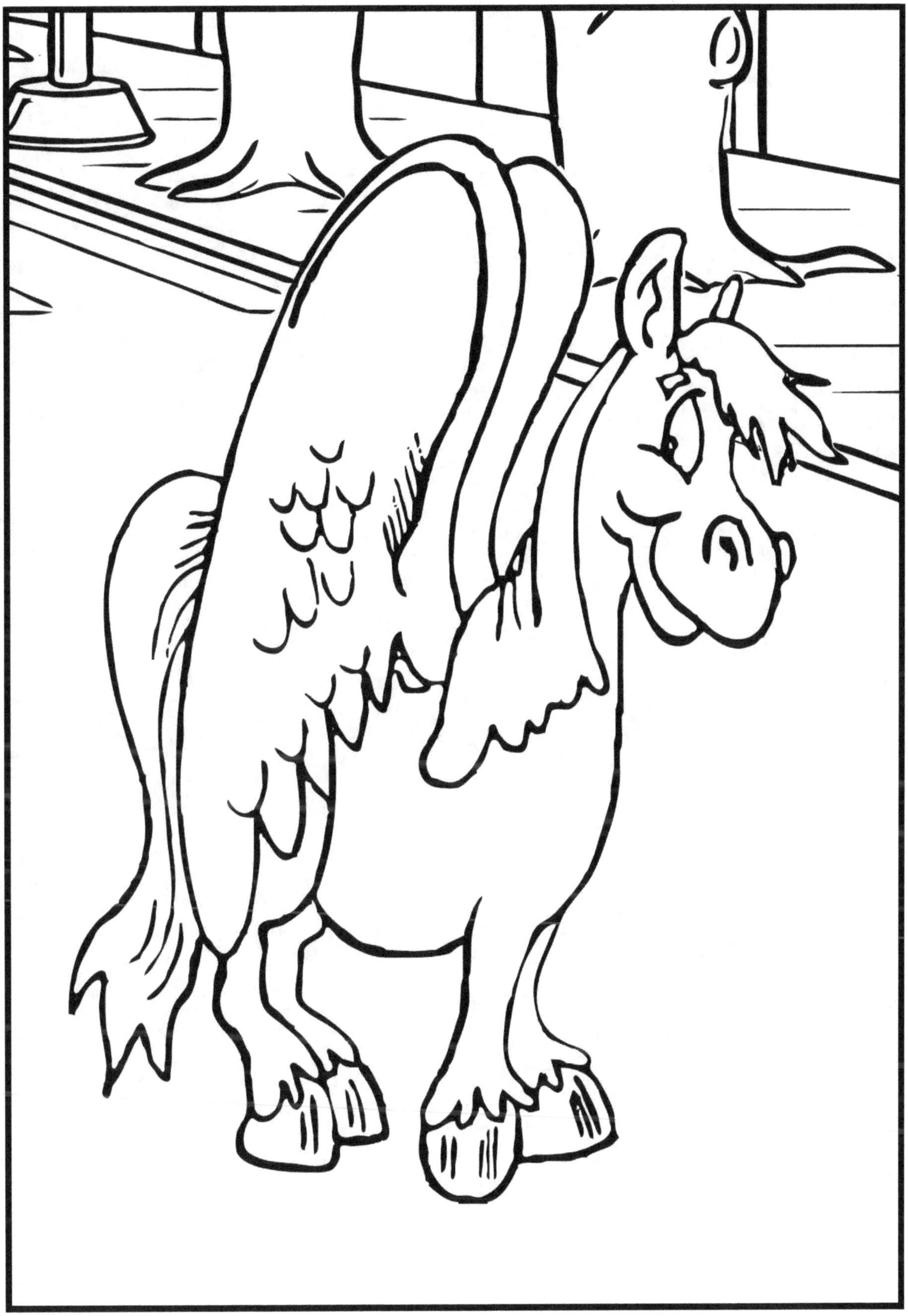

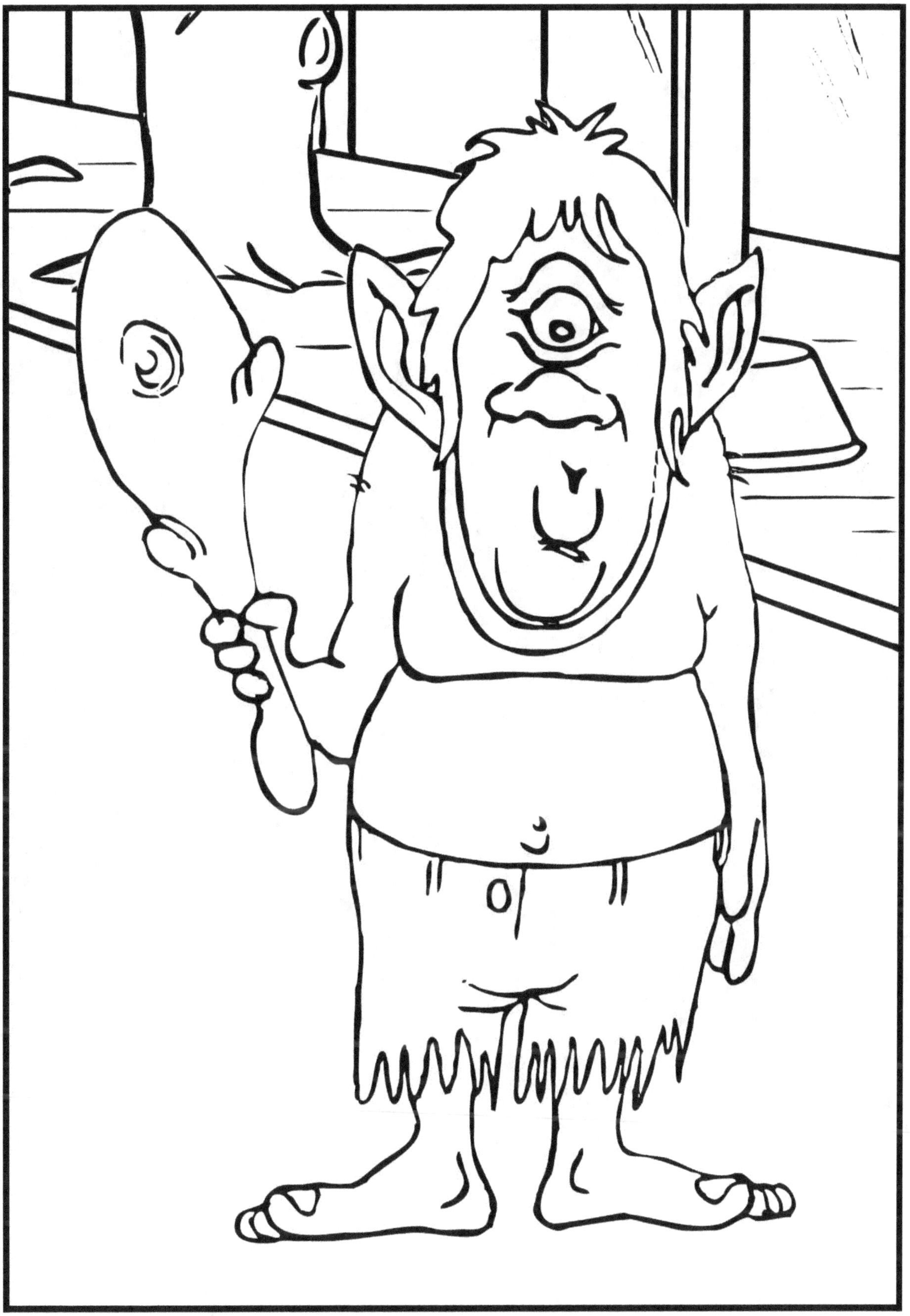

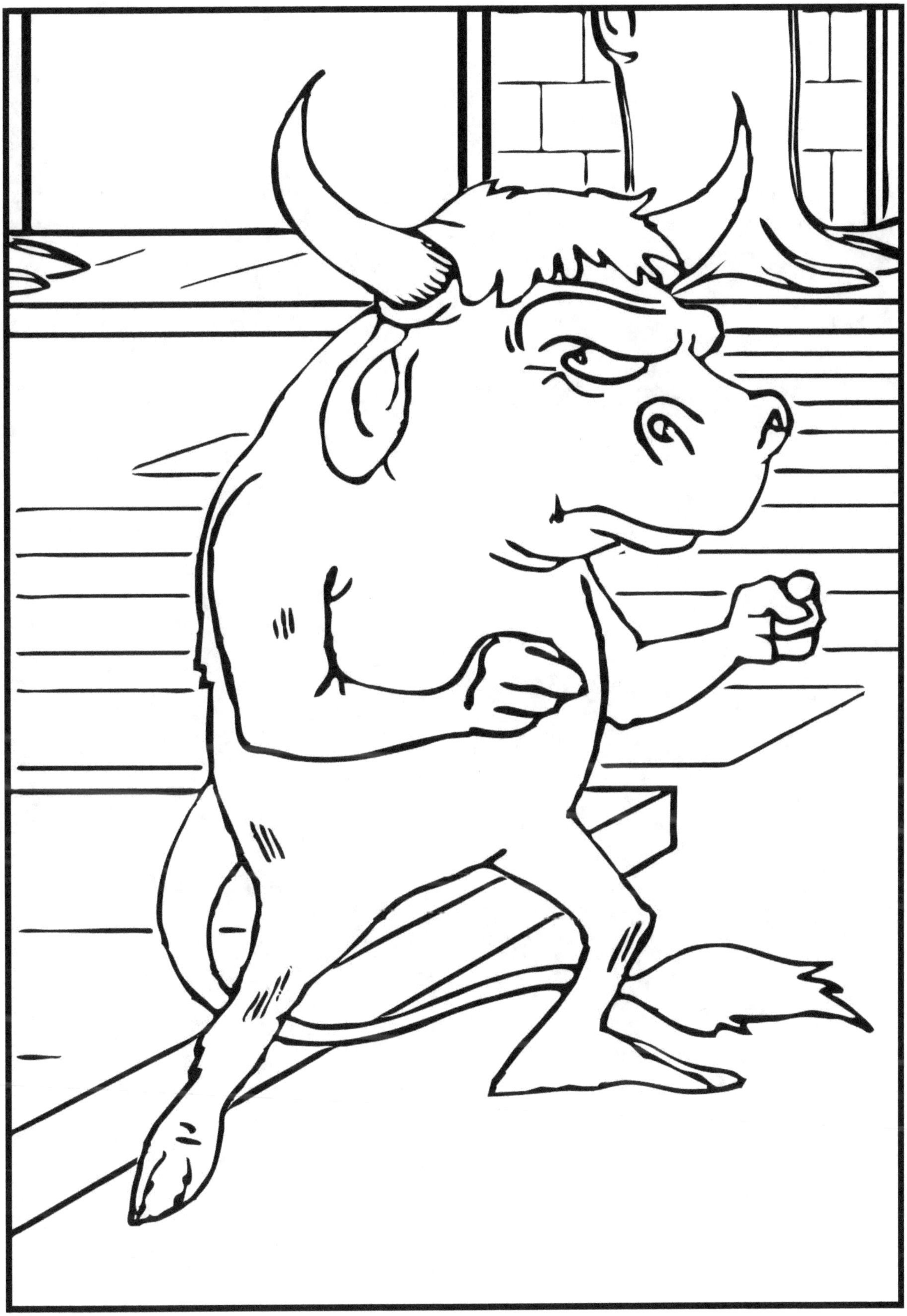

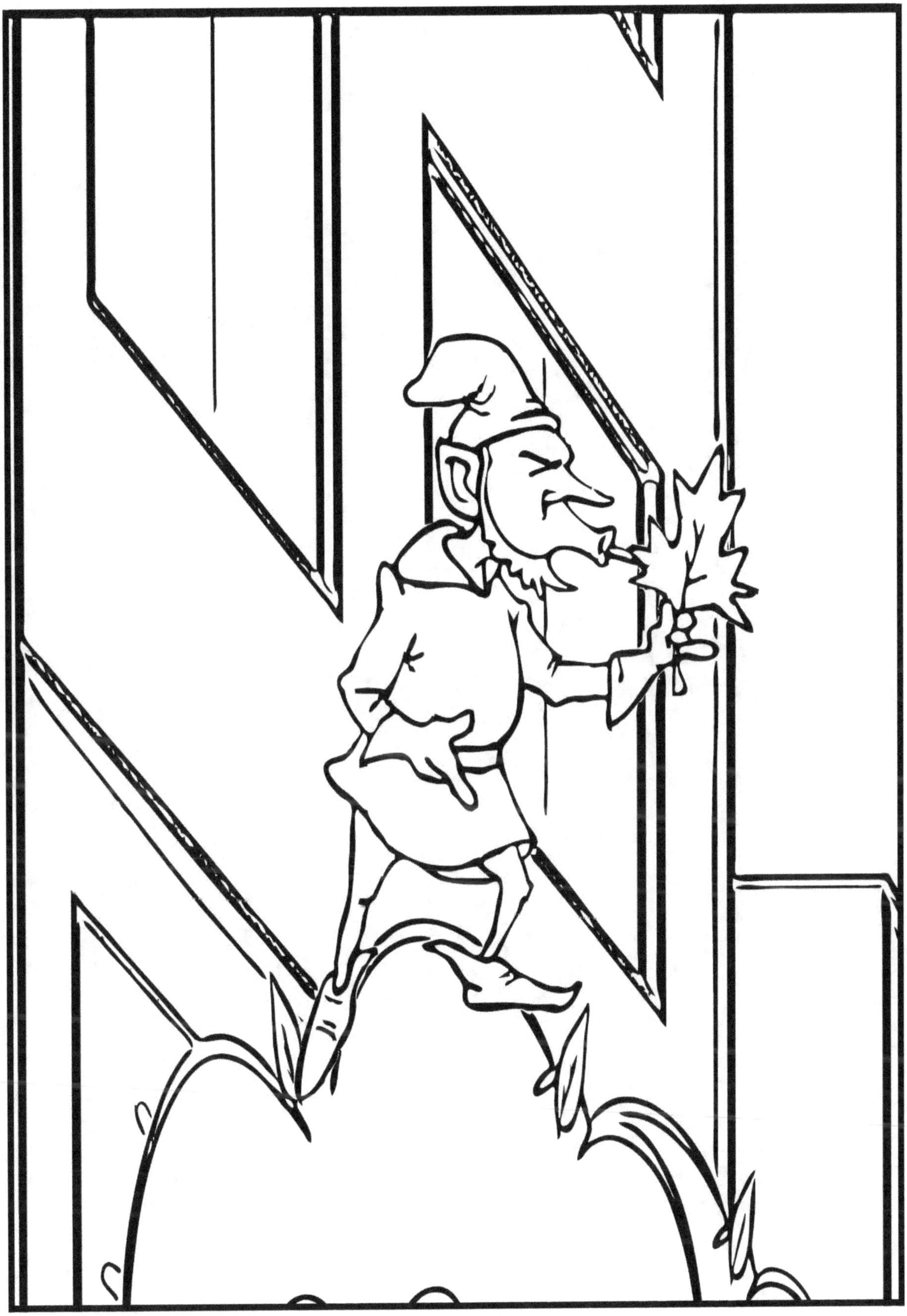

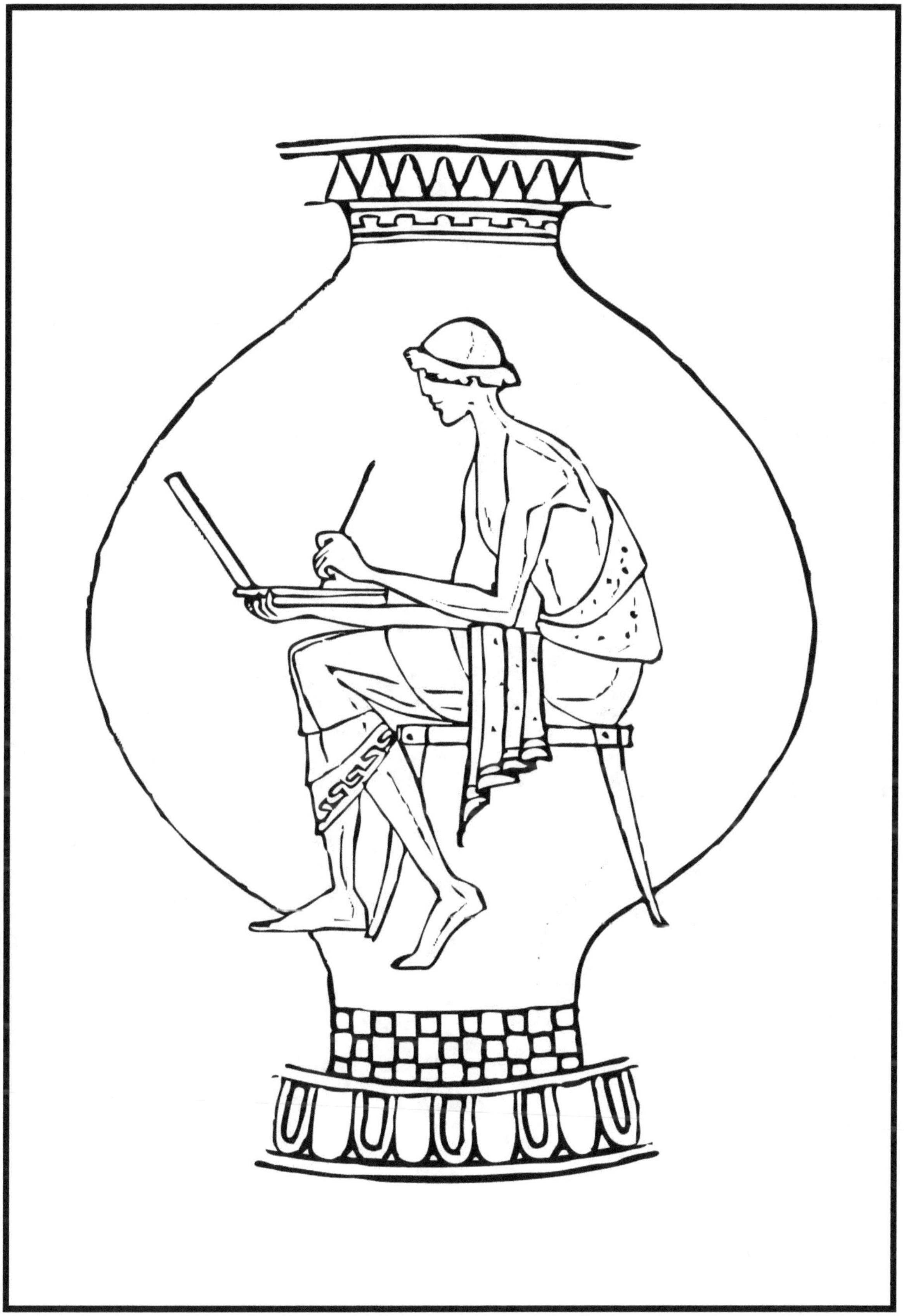

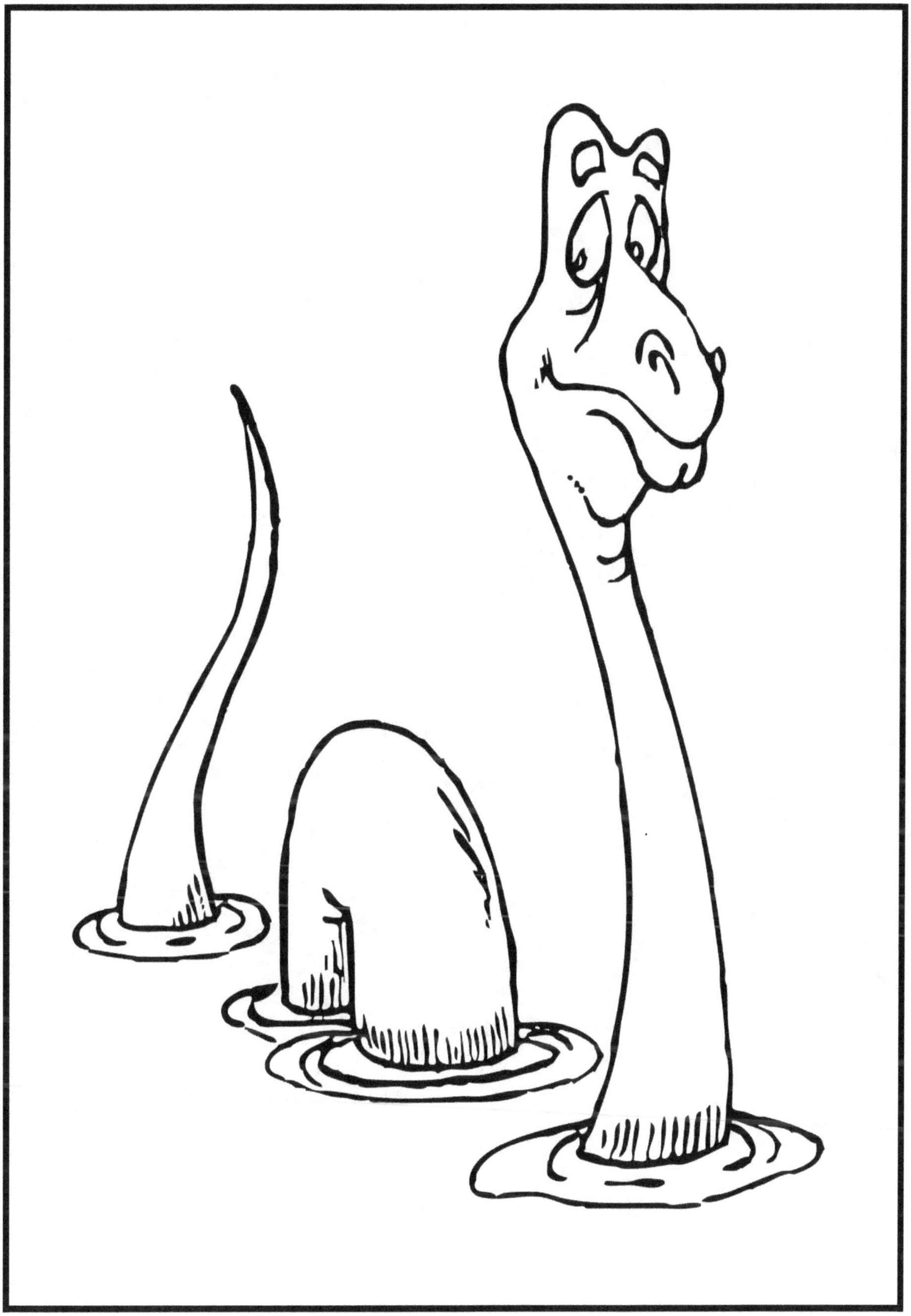

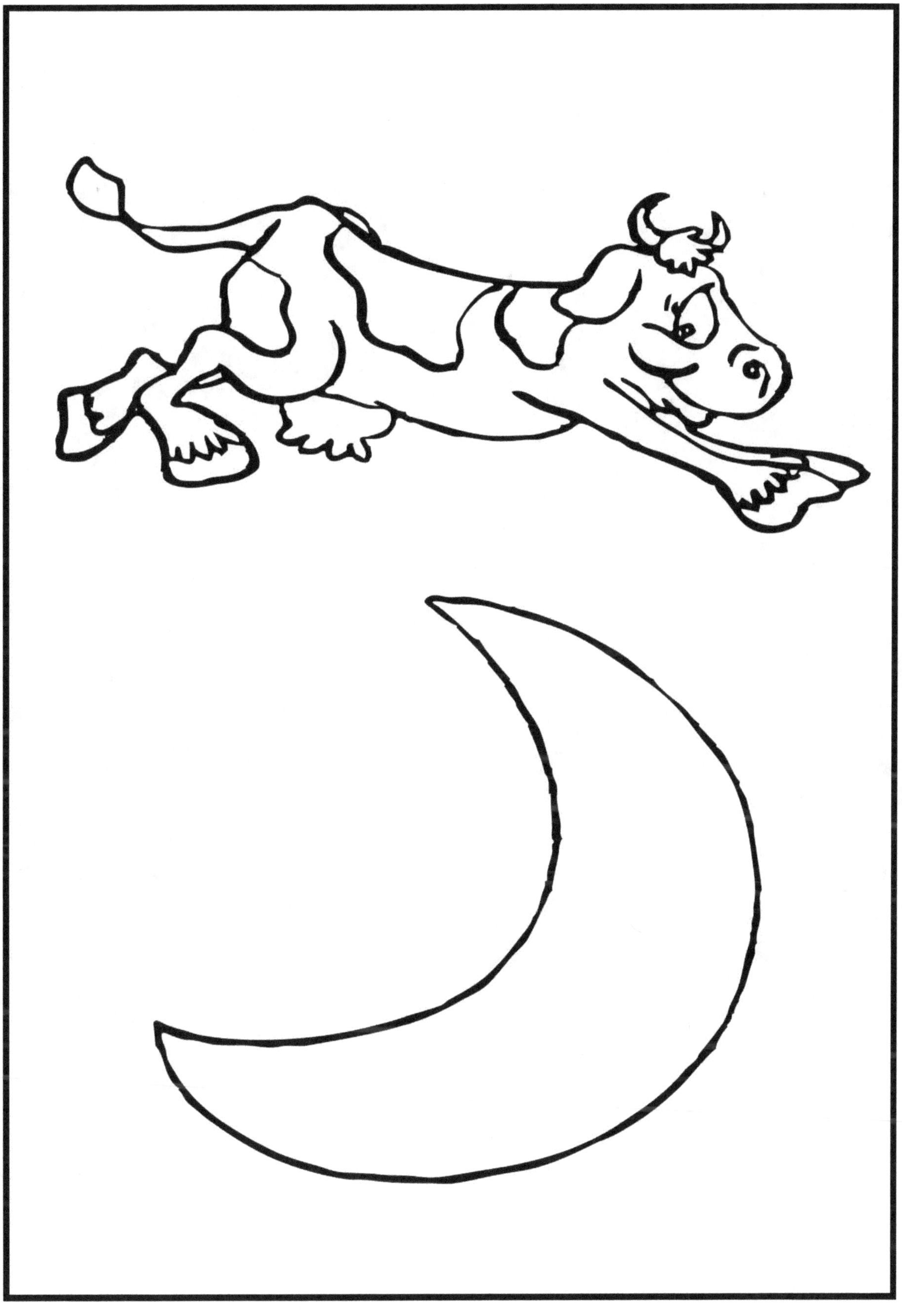

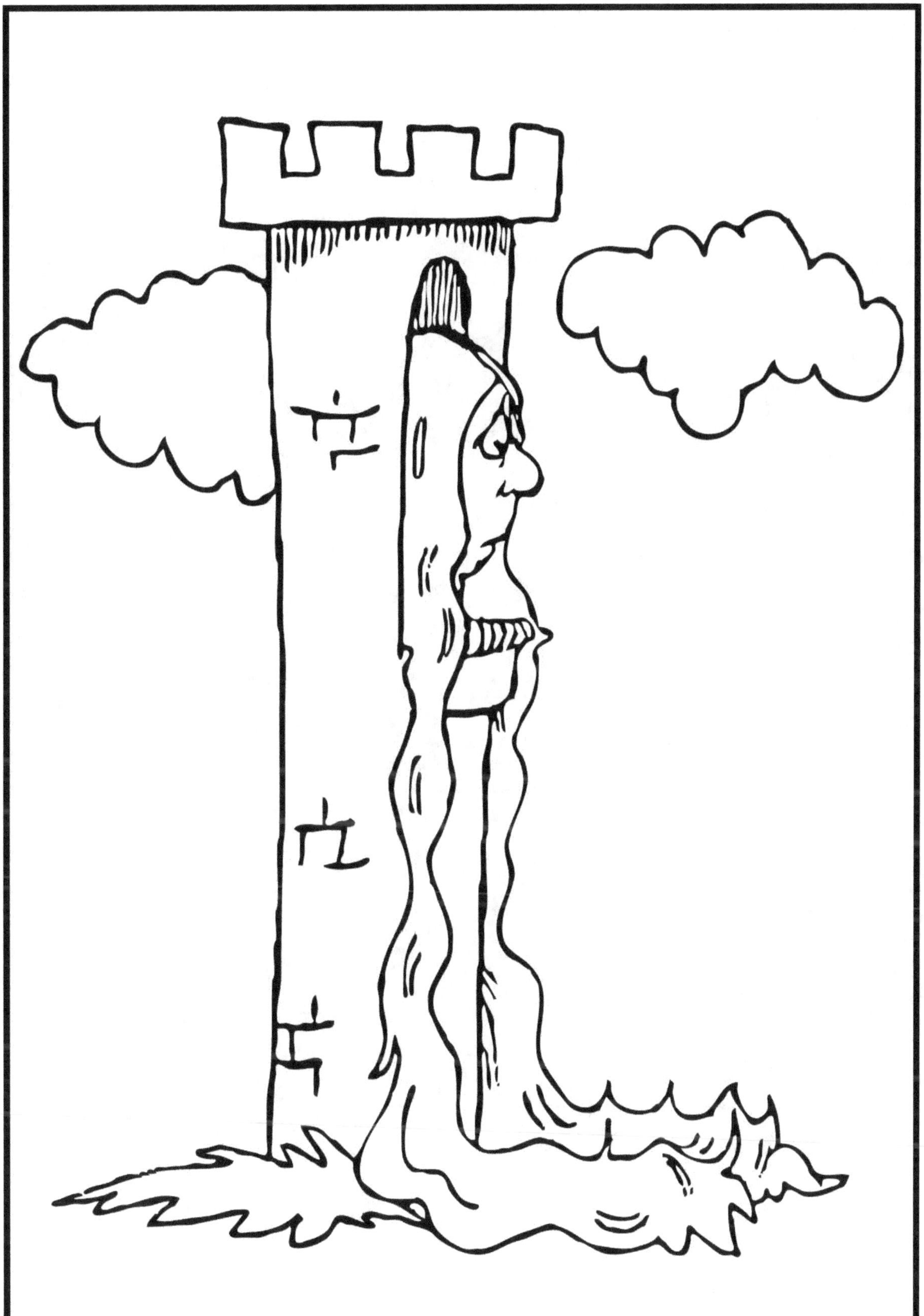

www.ingramcontent.com/pod-product-compliance
Lightning Source LLC
Chambersburg PA
CBHW081402170526
45166CB00010B/3169